THE BYZANTINE EMPIRE

A Complete Overview Of The Byzantine Empire History from Start to Finish

Eric Brown

© Copyright 2018 by Eric Brown

All rights reserved.

The following eBook is reproduced below with the goal of providing information that is as accurate and reliable as possible. Regardless, purchasing this eBook can be seen as consent to the fact that both the publisher and the author of this book are in no way experts on the topics discussed within and that any recommendations or suggestions that are made herein are for entertainment purposes only. Professionals should be consulted as needed prior to undertaking any of the action endorsed herein.

This declaration is deemed fair and valid by both the American Bar Association and the Committee of Publishers Association and is legally binding throughout the United States.

Furthermore, the transmission, duplication or reproduction of any of the following work including specific information will be considered an illegal act irrespective of if it is done electronically or in print. This extends to creating a secondary or tertiary copy of the work or a recorded copy and is only allowed with an expressed written consent from the Publisher. All additional rights reserved.

The information in the following pages is broadly considered to be truthful and accurate account of facts, and as such any inattention, use or misuse of the information in question by the reader will render any resulting actions solely under their purview. There are no scenarios in which the publisher or the original author of this work can be in any fashion deemed liable for any hardship or damages that may befall them after undertaking information described herein.

Additionally, the information in the following pages is intended only for informational purposes and should thus be thought of as universal. As befitting its nature, it is presented without assurance regarding its prolonged validity or interim quality. Trademarks that are mentioned are done without written consent and can in no way be considered an endorsement from the trademark holder.

Table of Contents

Introduction 5

Chapter 1: Creation, Division, and Standing Alone 6

Chapter 2: The Justinian Dynasty 13

Chapter 3: The Decline of the Empire and the Rise of Islam ... 20

Chapter 4: Resurgence Under the Macedonian Dynasty 27

Chapter 5: The Crusades and Their Impact 34

Chapter 6: The Fourth Crusade 41

Chapter 7: The Decline of the Empire and the Fall of
    Constantinople 47

Conclusion 53

Introduction

Congratulations on downloading *The Byzantine Empire*, and thank you for doing so.

The following chapters will discuss the rise and fall of one of the longest-lived empires in the history of the world. Though not as well-known today as the empire that spawned it, the Byzantine Empire stood for a thousand years as a continuation of the Roman Empire itself. From the founding of Constantinople by Emperor Constantine to the empire rising to its peaks under Justinian I and Basil II, down to its slow and tragic collapse following the sacking of Constantinople in 1204 CE, the entire history of the empire will be covered in this book.

The Byzantine Empire, having spent most of its history straddling Europe and Asia, had a tremendous impact on the culture of civilizations on both continents. As such, it should be as widely known as the other great empires in history. In part, this book intends to push a greater understanding of the second longest-lived empire in human history to a wider audience. From its cultural impact on the Ummayad Caliphate to its role in the Crusades, and to the impact of its collapse on Europe, the Byzantine Empire left its mark on multiple countries.

There are plenty of books on this subject on the market, so thanks again for choosing this one! Every effort was made to ensure it is full of as much useful information as possible. Please enjoy!

Chapter 1:
Creation, Division, and Standing Alone

It would be nearly impossible to discuss the history of the Byzantine Empire without first discussing the empire it succeeded: the Roman Empire. Founded in the final century before the Common Era, the Roman Empire was, at its peak, the most powerful political entity of its time. It controlled every territory in and around the Mediterranean Sea and spanned from Egypt to modern England. But the administrative system which had served it well during its initial two centuries eventually began to show some critical flaws.

It was under the reign of Emperor Diocletian that the idea of dividing the responsibilities of ruling the empire was first introduced. Diocletian came to power following a period of great strife for the empire known as the Crisis of the Third Century. It was a 50-year period following the death of Emperor Severus Alexander in 235 CE, which was marked by external invasions, civil wars, and economic stagnation. It briefly resulted in two large territories, the Gallic Empire and the Palmyrene Empire, breaking off from the empire. Though the empire was reunited under Emperor Aurelian, who reigned from 270-275 CE, it was not until the ascent of Diocletian in 284 CE that the empire truly recovered from the ordeal.

Due to coming to power following such a long period of crisis, Diocletian came to believe that the Roman Empire had simply outgrown the decentralized system of governance created by the first Emperor, Augustus. He sought to place more power in the hands of the Emperors to grant them the ability to rule more effectively. To this end, he instituted political reforms which ultimately marked the transition from the Principate period, wherein the Emperor was, in theory, considered first among equals amongst the senators, to the Dominate period, wherein the Emperors gradually took more and more power for themselves, often at the expense of the Senate.

The primary importance of this period to the later Byzantine Empire lay in the most vital reform made by Diocletian: the division of the empire into two distinct administrative zones. Initially naming Maximian as Caesar—or junior Emperor to his own Augustus or senior Emperor—in 285 CE, he went on to promote Maximian to Augustus the next year and declared that both men would choose their own Caesars to aid in the administration of the empire more directly. He took over the control of the Eastern Roman Empire, leaving the western half to Maximian. Though the Tetrarchy, or the "rule of four" as it was also known, did not last long following the retirement of its first two Augusti, it was important for having formalized the division between the culturally similar yet distinct eastern and western halves of the empire.

The simple fact that the pair retired was significant in itself, and the rarity of such an event likely contributed to the reasons why the system that Diocletian created failed to outlast him. It was a very old Roman concept—a public servant dedicating their time to truly serve the public and then retiring when they feel they could no longer work as well as they used to. It was actually seldom followed, and even the Roman Emperors who weren't killed either in battle against the empire's enemies or during civil conflicts more often than not died in office. The Tetrarchy did not live long past the reign of Diocletian because it had been him, in large part, who made the system effective: he was unusually dedicated to serving the public good over his own interests. Diocletian, in 305 CE, became the first Emperor to abdicate willingly. He then spent the final six years of his life retired in peace, tending a vegetable garden.

The reign of Constantine was by far the most important early influence on the later Byzantine Empire. Coming to power as Caesar in the west in 306 CE, he became the unquestioned Augustus by 312 CE. He ruled peacefully alongside the Augustus in the east Licinius for two years, but starting from 314 CE, the two became increasingly hostile rivals for power. In 321 CE, outright civil war broke out between them, and it ended in 324 CE following Constantine's victory at the Battle of Chrysopolis.

The civil war between the two emperors was seen at the time as a religious conflict between the Christian and Latin west and the pagan and Greek east. It was determined that to facilitate the reintegration of the Greek east into the empire, a new eastern capital needed to be established. To this end, Constantine chose the site of Byzantium and raised it as his own new capital. In 330 CE, Constantinople was established, marking the beginning of a permanent divide between the east and west that would be formalized some sixty-five years later.

Two other vital changes made by Constantine played a part in the history of the later-divided empire: the establishment of a hereditary succession tradition and the legalization of Christianity. Once it's been legalized, Christianity's leaders quickly moved to replace paganism as the dominant religion within the empire. Their success had been so rapid that by 395 CE, Emperor Theodosius I was able to outlaw paganism outright. Theodosius I was also able to leave the succession to his two sons without a significant civil conflict breaking out as a consequence—a testament to the success of the other major change made by Constantine.

Theodosius' sons, Arcadius and Honorius, inherited the Eastern and Western Roman Empires, respectively, and it was their reigns which marked the permanent division of the two halves. Arcadius and his successors would rule over the Eastern Roman Empire well beyond the fall of Rome itself. This official division merely served to formalize the divide which had always existed in one form or another. Though Latin was the language of administration and would remain so for centuries, there were a number of distinctions between the Eastern Roman Empire and the Western Roman Empire. Owing to its location and to the fact that it was once a part of the Macedonian Empire of Alexander the Great, the Eastern Roman Empire was more developed and urbanized than its western counterpart. This afforded them greater financial power and helped spare them from many of the tribulations which quickly followed for the west.

Their greater finances allowed the Eastern Roman Empire not only to employ mercenaries at a greater rate than did the west but also to more easily buy the services of figures like Attila the Hun. These things helped secure the east against collapse during the fifth century, the way the west did. The sack of Rome in 410 CE came as a devastating blow to the entire empire, and what followed for the west was nothing short of an ending. Over the next few decades, Rome bled power and territory at a staggering rate as the Germanic Tribes, referred to in Roman texts as Barbarians, ravaged the increasingly defenseless empire.

Another factor which helped the Eastern Roman Empire fare better was the nearly impenetrable defenses of Constantinople itself. Well-positioned along the Bosporus

Strait, Constantinople stood for centuries safe behind complex and well-built defenses. The walls fortified during the reign of Theodosius II in the mid-fifth century were not breached until 1204 CE. This combination of security and financial stability put the Eastern Empire in a position to weather the chaotic fifth century and emerge more or less unscathed, but this did not mean that they avoided danger altogether.

In addition to fortifying the walls of Constantinople, Theodosius II undertook a number of generally less successful measures against the Empire's foes. In 424 CE, after years of raids by the Huns, he negotiated an annual payment of three hundred and fifty pounds of gold in exchange for the Huns agreeing to end their raiding. When Attila and his brother Breda rose to prominence in 433 CE, the price was doubled to seven hundred pounds. This was a great example of both the empire's weakness and its ability to acquire funds when the need arose.

An attempt alongside the Western Roman Empire to repel a Vandal invasion of Roman North Africa in 439 CE failed utterly, but in 443 CE, when two returning armies were ambushed and destroyed by the Huns, the sudden increased danger from the Huns meant that further negotiation was needed. In a humiliating settlement, the Eastern Roman Empire agreed to increase their tribute to twenty-one hundred pounds of gold, a sixfold increase over what it had been just twenty years prior. But while this sudden increase in danger to the Eastern Roman Empire was significant, it was far from the only change they underwent during that difficult century.

By the time Attila the Hun died in 453 CE, the Byzantine Empire had already established significant contacts with a number of tribes that had come to the empire from the east. The Alans, a nomadic people originally from a region in modern Iran, had settled in such numbers and been given such power within the empire that the Alanic general Aspar came to hold great influence over three successive Eastern Roman Emperors. That the last of these three, Leo I, had had him killed in 471 CE is largely irrelevant given how common, in general, such power struggles were at the time. What mattered most was the fact that the tribes, which had devastated the western empire over the previous century, had become important enough within it in their own right to be entrusted with positions of power.

The practice of using so-called Barbarians to fend off other tribes was hardly unique to the Eastern Roman Empire, but they possessed greater capital with which to employ them. In 476 CE, when the Gothic-Roman general Odoacer deposed the final Western Roman Emperor, Romulus Augustulus, the Eastern Roman Empire was left with little choice but to work with him until he betrayed the Eastern Emperor Zeno by supporting a rival claimant. Zeno's solution to that problem came not in the form of raising Roman armies and reconquering Italy but in seeking the aid of Ostrogothic leader Theodoric the Great, to whom Zeno gave the order to kill and replace Odoacer in 493 CE.

The significance of that event is twofold. On the one hand, it demonstrated that the Eastern Roman Empire was still deeply interested in the affairs of the west, even after the Western Roman Empire had died out completely. On the other hand, it shows that though the interest was there, the power was not. In addition, although Constantinople was wealthy, it was not the military power that it needed to be if it was to support its interest in the west. Though both of these factors would change in time, with the Byzantine Empire both growing stronger and growing less interested in the Latin West, these changes, especially the latter, would take time to play out. By the end of the fifth century, the Eastern Roman Empire was still deeply tied to the west culturally, and the golden age it would experience during the Justinian Dynasty was brought about in part because of this continued desire to hold onto tradition and the greater empire that had once existed.

Still, the ability of the Justinian Emperors to build that golden age had been possible, in part, due to the competent reign of the final Leonid Emperor Anastasius I. His reign, from 491 to 518 CE, was characterized both by stability and by financial reforms. He completed Constantine's efforts to reform the coinage of the empire by introducing a new, strictly weighted copper coin for general use. He also reformed the taxation system, doing away with the much-despised Chrysargyron Tax. His financial reforms left the empire in excellent shape, with a treasury containing over three hundred thousand pounds of gold at the time of his death. By the sixth century, the Eastern Empire was in a position to retake the western imperial holdings and possessed the clear desire to do so.

Chapter 2:
The Justinian Dynasty

The Justinian Dynasty is commonly said to have reigned over a golden age of the Byzantine Empire. Beginning with the reign of Emperor Justin I which started in 518 CE, the dynasty lasted until the death of Emperor Maurice in 602 CE. This dynasty saw the Byzantine Empire reach its greatest territorial scope. As important as that was, however, the deep cultural change that took place during the period was even more significant. When Justin I took the throne, he was largely illiterate and spoke little to no Greek. He surrounded himself with educated advisors, including his nephew and successor Justinian I, to counteract this lack. Still, the simple fact that a man who barely spoke Greek could become the Byzantine Emperor spoke of how "Latin" the empire still was. In contrast, by the time the first Emperor of the Heraclian Dynasty reigned in the early seventh century, Latin as a language was only being used ceremonially.

This transition was in part the result of the Byzantine Empire's initial success in reclaiming many of the western territories, as well as their subsequent loss of the same. At the start, however, the Justinian Dynasty benefited from relative peace and stability, which lasted until the final years of Justin's reign. The most important accomplishment of his reign was the mending of relations with the Papacy.

Justin himself was a devout Orthodox Christian which, in the sixth century, meant that he was in line with the official positions of the Papacy. Prior Eastern Roman Emperors had been Monophysites, a Christian group who disagreed with the Papacy over whether or not Jesus could be both divine and human in nature, believing that he could not have been. This dispute, known as the Acacian Schism, had been an issue for over three decades by the time Justin I and Patriarch John of Cappadocia formally ended it in 519 CE.

As significant as this was to Christendom at the time, it paled in comparison to the accomplishments of the man who succeeded Justin I: Justinian I. Justinian I was a man of great focus when it came to issues that mattered to him, but he was one who disregarded the things that did not. He cared little for class distinction, having chosen to marry a lower-class woman by the name of Theodora who had worked as an actress and a prostitute. He did this only after his uncle made it legally possible for him to do so in 525 CE, just two years before his own reign began. When he took the throne, he inherited a war with the Sassanid Empire of Persia, which had begun in the final years of his uncle's reign. When his general Belisarius suffered a defeat at the Battle of Callinicum in 531 CE, Justinian quickly took advantage of the unrelated death of the Sassanid Emperor to negotiate peace with his successor. At the cost of eleven thousand pounds of gold, Justinian signed the "Eternal Peace" agreement of 532 CE. His focus simply was not on the east but rather lay directed toward the west.

The same year that peace with the Sassanids was secured, Justinian was forced to deal with a domestic threat that nearly ended his reign then and there. The Nika Riots were a response to Justinian's habit of appointing ministers who were efficient and effective at their jobs but who were unpopular with the people. Much of life in Constantinople at the time revolved around associations known as "demes" which supported competitors in various sports, particularly chariot racing. These demes were essentially sports associations, but they operated quite differently from the ones we know in the modern day. Not only would members of demes support their faction in sporting events, that faction would also have political positions which they would often shout at the Emperor between races at the formal events. Over the years, these demes evolved into informal entities which were one part political party, one part street gang.

As one can imagine from that description, it was not uncommon for brawls to break out during sports events and for minor riots to occur as a consequence. If any murders took place, the law stated that the murderers would be hanged. In 532 CE, such an event happened, and two of the murderers—one from the blue faction and one from the green faction—happened to escape. As their respective factions demanded that they be pardoned, Justinian, who was in the midst of negotiating with the Sassanids and had raised taxes leading up to the riots, feared the possibility of chaos and commuted their sentences.

At the next race, however, this move proved not to be enough, and the formerly bitter rival factions found themselves united against the Emperor. With shouts of "Nika," meaning "victory" which gave the riots their name, they besieged the palace. Justinian, it is said, considered fleeing, but he was dissuaded by Theodora and hatched a plan instead. He sent a eunuch by the name of Narsus out with a bag of gold. He had the eunuch give gold to the leaders of the blue faction as well as a reminder that Justinian supported them—on the other hand, the man the rioters were trying to replace him with, Hypatius, supported the green faction.

This turned out to be enough to persuade them as the blue faction members quickly abandoned the green faction members who, suddenly bereft of the numbers they had enjoyed before, found themselves at the mercy of Justinian's generals. A total of thirty thousand people are said to have been killed that week, and half the city burned down, including its most prominent church the Hagia Sophia. Justinian would use this as an opportunity to rebuild the city—in particular, the Hagia Sophia—and make it his, further securing his own power through the bloodshed.

Justinian's greatest obsession lay with the west, in the lands of the former Western Roman Empire. Historians often refer to him as the "last Roman" for this reason, as much of his reign ended up dedicated to partially successful efforts to reconquer the western territories. This started with the Vandalic War, a war with a Germanic tribe called the Vandals which had taken much of Rome's territory in North Africa during the collapse of the Western Empire. It was the first and arguably most successful of Justinian's wars of reconquest. Lasting from 533-534 CE, it resulted in the crushing defeat of the Vandals and the conquest of the land. Though it was costly and it ultimately took until 548 CE to fully pacify the region, the endeavor was a success.

Contrasting this was his war to reclaim Italy which, though similarly successful in the 530s, dragged on for far longer and ended up being significantly more costly. Belisarius was again dispatched with an army, that time around with the intention to reclaim the former heartland of the Roman Empire and the city itself from the Ostrogoths. Having fallen since the days of Theoderic, the Ostrogoths of Italy under the reign of Theodahad were in a poor position to hold out against the invading Byzantines. Though it lasted longer than the Vandalic War, taking the Byzantines from 535 until 540 CE to conquer, it was initially a great victory for Justinian.

These initial victories slowly gave way to problems, despite how much they may have appeared to be great in the beginning. For one thing, Justinian's westward focus left him vulnerable when the Sassanids broke the Eternal Peace in 540 CE. Though the Byzantines lost no territory in the sporadic fighting that occurred during the following twenty-two years, it did serve to further drain the empire's resources. When the Ostrogothic resurgence began in 541 CE, it took another thirteen years of fighting to retake and secure the Italian peninsula. In all, the campaigns were a success, and Justinian succeeded in securing territory that stretched as far as the coast of modern-day Spain. The cost, however, was tremendous.

By the end of Justinian's reign, though the borders of the Byzantine Empire had reached the greatest extent that they ever would, the treasury which had been overflowing with gold when his uncle first began his reign was empty. The empire was left overtaxed in more ways than one with its resources stretched thin and its people chaffing under the increased tax dues. The main problem that the Emperor faced during his reign was an inability to realize that his good fortune had not continued past the 530s. It would take some time before the Byzantines lost everything he had spent his reign retaking, but before terribly long, they would.

One accomplishment of Justinian's reign that lasted well beyond its inception was the Code of Justinian. Another example of Justinian's ability to focus on matters which were important to him, the code was compiled to remedy a problem he had noted in the way Roman Law was handled in the Byzantine Empire. When he came to the throne, he almost immediately ordered a compilation of imperial constitutions. Rome had existed for so long and had gone through so many often-dramatic changes in leadership that it had numerous constitutions and laws in effect, which were often handled in different ways by different courts. Justinian saw the bureaucratic mess that this resulted in and thus undertook to curb the number of court proceedings which occurred in a given year by reducing the number of constitutions.

The process itself took five years to complete, and by 534 CE, the entire code had been promulgated throughout the empire. Though initially a success and done in three parts as he had intended, Justinian, later on, discovered the need to introduce new laws. All in all, however, the project had its intended effect, and the code remained in place for centuries following his death. It was even used in the 11th century by western scholars as a source for older Roman law.

The three other Emperors of the Justinian Dynasty invariably dealt with the aftermath of Justinian's ambition. Justin II sought to continue his predecessor's successes but had neither the funds nor the talent to do so. His realization of just how dire the empire's financial situation was had led him to suspend payment to the neighboring Avars, ending a truce which had been in place for two decades. The Avars, in response, allied with the Lombards, who went on to take over nearly all of Italy outside of the major cities and Sicily. Though he succeeded in holding back the forces of the Avars, his troubles with the Sassanids in the late sixth century resulted in the loss of the vital fortress of Dara in Syria and pushed Justin II over the edge. He abdicated a broken man and was succeeded by Tiberius II.

Tiberius was a more capable Emperor, but he still faced the same central issues plaguing the empire in that period. Having started his reign in 574 CE, he had, by 579 CE, already noted that his forces were complete overextended. Though he fared well against the Avars, the Byzantine's continuing struggles against the Sassanids made it impossible to deal with them with any degree of finality. By 582 CE, there seemed to be no end in sight for the Persian conflict, and Tiberius himself was dying, having eaten food that was either poisoned or simply ill-prepared. With no son to leave the empire to, the throne passed to his primary general, Maurice, the final Emperor of the Justinian Dynasty.

Maurice enjoyed the longest reign of any Emperor in the dynasty save for Justinian himself. Despite this and the numerous military victories that he had, both before he took the throne and after, he was the only one of them who was deposed. Though he was a truly capable general, he suffered from the lack of readily available funds in the face of frequent military campaigns, just as his predecessors had been. He was the only Justinian Emperor to truly defeat the Sassanids in 591 CE, ending up with a peace deal that actually saw the Persian nation cede territory to Byzantium instead of a deal based on Byzantine tribute payments. The price of this, however, was the need to cut military wages by a quarter in 588 CE, a move which provoked a mutiny which he barely managed to quell.

By 602 CE, though he had been one of the most successful Emperors the Byzantines had had in recent decades, Maurice had become wildly unpopular. Another military coup turned out to be insurmountable, and it ended in the death of Maurice and his six sons. A military officer named Phocas was crowned Emperor, and the military moved to secure his new reign, but it came at a significant cost. The Sassanids, realizing what an opportunity the sudden instability and loss of a capable leader meant for the Byzantines, took that chance to start a war which would last for 26 years and exhaust both sides at a truly critical juncture.

Chapter 3: The Decline of the Empire and the Rise of Islam

To understand just how disastrous Phocas' reign was for the Byzantine Empire, it is important to understand just what it represented. Though for much of its history, the Roman Empire had been subject to significant succession crises, since the fall of Rome, the Eastern Roman Empire had been relatively stable in that respect. Issues such as the Nika Riots had been quelled, and there hadn't been any major civil conflicts beyond that—other than a short problem in the fifth century between Emperor Zeno and his brother-in-law Basilicus. The deposition of Maurice and the ascent of Phocas thus represented a struggle that the empire had not experienced for decades and, as a result, had been quite ill-equipped to handle.

Maurice had defeated the Sassanids in part by helping the exiled prince Khosrow, who would become Khosrow II, to take the Persian throne. In exchange for this, the Byzantine Empire had been ceded significant territories in northeastern Mesopotamia and the Caucasus region and had its annual tribute revoked. With the death of Maurice, Khosrow had an opportunity to attack the Byzantine Empire both to avenge his old ally Maurice and to retake the territory he had only reluctantly agreed to give up in the first place. It would be the final and most devastating war between the two empires, and it would ultimately leave both exhausted and vulnerable.

The Byzantines may well have done better against the initial assaults by the Sassanids had Phocas proven himself a more competent leader. Given that he was just a centurion before he was elevated to Emperor, Phocas had no connection to the local elite, and he distrusted them completely. To get around this, he practiced nepotism on a scale beyond the norm for the period, appointing his brothers and nephew to various posts within Constantinople. Adding to this was his general paranoia. He came to believe that his position was precarious and, as a consequence, spent much of his time putting down conspiracies—both real and imagined—and purging his enemies. He devoted so much of his eight-year reign to this pursuit that his response to the Sassanids was ineffective at best.

Within six years, the Sassanid forces had come to occupy Syria, Mesopotamia, and most of Asia Minor. When Narses, a Maurice loyalist, defected, Phocas invited him to Constantinople with the promise of safety and then had him burned alive. Such conduct would have likely resulted in rebellion even if the empire hadn't been facing an existential threat in the form of the Sassanids. In this case, it came in the form of Heraclius the Elder, a powerful Exarch of Carthage; his cousin Nicetas; and his son Heraclius. They started their effort to overthrow the blatant tyrant in 609 CE by cutting off the supply of grain to Constantinople while they assembled their army and navy. The following year, through invading by land and sea, they seized the city after a two-day siege, executed Phocas, and had Heraclius crowned Emperor.

Immediately after Heraclius took the throne, the Sassanids enjoyed their greatest victories. The ancient cities of Damascus and Jerusalem fell to the Persian forces in 613 CE, and the True Cross, the cross said to have been used in the Crucifixion of Jesus Christ was stolen. With one of the holiest cities in the Christian tradition occupied and possibly the religion's holiest relic taken back to the Sassanid capital of Ctesiphon, Heraclius' response took on the form of a Holy War.

Before he could start his counteroffensive in earnest, however, Heraclius was left with the difficult task of reorganizing a severely weakened empire.

With the Sassanids having taken the Levant and Egypt, the Byzantine Empire was left without much of its usual grain supply. It also lost significant tax revenue due to the loss of the provinces. To deal with this crisis, Heraclius imposed severe budget cuts on the entire administration, halving the pay of government officials and enforcing extreme fines on anyone who committed acts of corruption. He also devalued the currency, ordering the creation of lighter coins to ease the financial burden of the state. While in other times, such actions may well have sparked a rebellion against the government, the loss of Jerusalem and the holy relics had created in the people of the Byzantine Empire a religious fervor which made them more than willing to put up with such discomfort if it meant dealing with the Persians.

Heraclius' counteroffensive began in 622 CE, with his armies marching across Anatolia to push out the occupying Persians. The Chronicles are unclear as to what truly transpired, but what is known is that in the autumn of 622 CE, he won a decisive victory over the Sassanid general Shahrbaraz in eastern Anatolia. This served to push the Persian forces out of the region and give the empire temporary relief.

Though Heraclius offered peace to Khosrow in 624 CE, his offer was rejected, and he ended up invading Persia. Traveling through the Caucasus region, he chose to spend the winter in Caucasian Albania in the east of the region to gather more troops and be ready to assault the Persian mainland in the spring. Khosrow sent multiple armies after him in that region, but as fortified as Heraclius' position was and as capable as he was as a general, they made little progress.

Shahrbaraz, in particular, fared poorly when, following the infiltration of two supposed deserters from Heraclius' camp, he was led to believe that Heraclius was attempting to flee. Sending half his forces to the position where the fraudulent traitors had said that he was moving toward, he soon found himself ambushed instead. With his army destroyed, Shahrbaraz, according to the accounts of the time, barely managed to flee, leaving behind his troops, his resources, and apparently his clothing

With his enemy's primary general naked and alone, fleeing to the nearest Persian fortress, Heraclius managed to secure his position farther in, spending the rest of the winter in Trebizond. While Heraclius kept his forces in the Caucasus region and northern Persia, Khosrow sought to force him to pull back by sending his armies around his foe to assault Constantinople itself. Allying with the Turkish Avars, his generals sought to attempt a two-pronged siege of the city from both the European side and through crossing the Bosporus Strait. This siege in 626 CE ultimately failed, however, owing to the city's notorious defenses and the Byzantine navy's complete control of the Aegean sea, Bosporus Strait, and Sea of Marmara.

While Heraclius did divert some of his forces to the city to reinforce it, he was left with more than enough troops to raid the Persian heartland. The Persian raids culminated with the Battle of Ninevah. As he returned home, having devastated most of the Persian armies, he encountered an army under the command of the Sassanid commander Rhahzadh near the ruins of Ninevah. The battle was a bloody affair with an estimated six thousand Sassanid troops dying alongside their commander. It was a significant victory for the Byzantines as it left the Persians with no viable armies left to throw against the

Byzantines. What remained of the Persian forces overthrew Khosrow and replaced him with his son Kavadh II.

With a new Sassanid leader to negotiate with, Heraclius offered a deal which saw the restoration of the lost Byzantine territory and the True Cross in exchange for no harsh penalties being issued against the defeated power. In truth, each side was virtually as exhausted as the other, and Heraclius had no desire to press his luck. With the deal agreed to, the two sides left to lick their wounds, each unaware that they would not get much of a chance.

Happening almost in complete chronological parallel to the final Byzantine-Sassanid War was Muhammad's rise to power and subsequent death. Though the prophet of Islam never expanded his territory past the Arabian Peninsula, the same could not be said of his successors. The Rashidun Caliphate, the name given at the time to the first four Caliphs following Muhammad's death in 632 CE, had overseen a quarter century of near-constant expansion at an incredible rate. Whether one wants to call it luck, divine providence, or serendipity, the fact that the Arabs began their expansion at the exact same time when their most powerful neighbors had just finished destroying one another certainly turned out to be favorable for them. By the end of Rashidun Caliphate in 661 CE, their territory already spanned from modern Tunisia to modern Afghanistan.

For the Byzantines, this meant the immediate loss of Egypt, much of North Africa, the Levant, and Mesopotamia, as these found themselves completely unable to withstand the frequent raids by the battle-hardened and well-supplied Arab armies. In this, the seventh century was for the Byzantines one characterized by terrible tribulation and change. They went from being an empire which spanned from Iberia to the Levant to one which was confined to Anatolia, the Balkans, and fragments of Italy. This brought with it a number of social changes as well.

In particular, the Byzantine Empire quickly ruralized as the loss of grain-producing regions such as Egypt made supplying large cities impossible. The same thing happened in the Western Roman Empire over the course of the fifth century as the collapse of the old trade routes forced people to abandon the cities. This, in turn, forced the Byzantine Empire to make the transition from a Late Antique empire to a Medieval state.

Historians argue that another consequence of this transition marks the moment when it is more correct to classify the Byzantine Empire as a successor state, such as those which developed in the west, rather than a continuation of Rome itself. Given how much Roman territory they lost, one could make that argument on those grounds alone, but it goes beyond that. Heraclius was the Emperor who introduced Greek as the official language of the empire. Considering that among the Emperors of the previous dynasty, only Maurice had been a native Greek speaker, that was an enormous change to make, and yet it happened. It speaks to a growing distance between Constantinople and their Latin Roman roots, even as they would continue to claim their status as Rome's continuation right until the end.

One aspect of the growing cultural split between the east and the west was the position that the Eastern Church would take on the issue of icons. Iconoclasm is the banning of religious icons for fear that using them in moments of worship can lead to worship of the icons themselves rather than of God. Beginning during the reign of Leo III of the Isaurian Dynasty, the practice of tearing down religious icons became official policy in 730 CE. The Western Church disagreed with them so strongly about the issue of iconoclasm that it influenced their decision to distance themselves from Constantinople.

The Byzantine Papacy refers to the period 537 to 752 CE wherein the Papacy in Rome required the approval of the Emperor for the appointment of new Popes. This was the result of Justinian I choosing to appoint three Popes over the course of his reign following the conquest of Italy from the Ostrogoths. The Papacy put up with this with very little complaint because they had been, for a time, happy to be closer to the continued Roman Empire. The issue of Iconoclasm was one of the few major differences between them at that point in history—few people in the west opposed icons, and the papacy itself was very much in favor of them. By 752 CE, the Papacy and Constantinople were very much divided due to numerous factors.

The Muslim Conquests took up much of Constantinople's time and energy, diverting their attention away from Italy where the Lombards grew increasingly powerful and threatening to Rome. By the turn of the century, the Papacy had approved a new Emperor in the west for the first time in over three centuries, and Charlemagne and his successors became for Rome far more favorable option than the Emperors in the east.

Chapter 4: Resurgence Under the Macedonian Dynasty

Though the Byzantine Empire reached its territorial zenith under Justinian I, it reached its true peak in terms of power under the Macedonian Dynasty. Under the Reign of Basil I and his dynastic successors, it grew to once again become a force to be reckoned with in the eastern Mediterranean. In what some have termed the Macedonian Renaissance, its culture thrived as well, with education reviving and ancient texts being copied for distribution to the growing cities.

By mid-ninth century, the Byzantine Empire had changed its administrative structure significantly. With the loss of territory during the initial Muslim Conquests, the old trade system had been disrupted, and while this mostly resulted in the decline of the cities in the beginning, it also resulted in the reorganization of the provincial system. In place of the provinces which had been the administrative divisions put in place by Constantine and Diocletian, the Theme System of military administration took form. It was similar in a way to the feudal system of western Europe which developed after the fall of Rome, as the land was divided into plots used by soldiers and their families in exchange for service. The primary difference was that the land remained under the control of the Imperium, and the Emperor could and often did remove and appoint administrators at will.

It was from this system that Basil I emerged as a simple peasant before climbing his way up the ranks under the reign of Michael III. When he took power himself in 867 CE, he quickly proved himself to be a capable—if mildly unstable—ruler. Though he warred successfully against the Paulicians and the Arabs, managing to briefly retake the island of Cyprus, most of Sicily was lost during his reign. His foreign policy, though ambitious and often westward-focused, was not the most notable part of his reign: where he truly shined as a leader was on the domestic front, and he came to be known as the second Justinian for his legislative work. The collection of laws he compiled came to be known as the Basilika, a collection of sixty books. It was the most extensive legal project undertaken since the reign of Justinian I.

The religious tension between Constantinople and Rome was one thing that Basil attempted to remedy. His solution was to exile the then-Patriarch of Constantinople Photios and to replace him with Ignatius, whom Rome favored, to curry favor with them without giving up much ground. This, however, backfired—ten years later, in 877 CE, Ignatius died and was replaced again by Photios. Photios' reclamation of his post resulted in an informal but undeniable split between the churches in the east and west, which helped pave the way for the eventual formal split in the 11th century.

Under Basil's reign, a culture of letters formed throughout the empire, and educated men began writing to each other to spread ideas and consult with one another; this is similar to the culture which developed during the later, more famous Renaissance. Though this cultural flowering continued during the reigns of Basil's immediate successors, his already limited military successes did not. Under the reign of Basil I, Boris I of Bulgaria had allied the church in his country with Constantinople instead of Rome. While this had been a boon for Basil, it quickly became clear in the years and decades following his death that the Bulgarians had no interest in being subservient to the Byzantines.

Under Simeon I, the Bulgarians waged two wars against the Byzantines, first in 894-896 CE, and then again in 913-927 CE. Both were successes for Simeon, with the first gaining them the Bulgarian kingdom territory in Thrace and the second gaining Simeon himself very reluctant recognition as a fellow Emperor by Constantinople. The situation with the Bulgarians would not change until the final quarter of the century, and the tribute payments that the Byzantines were forced to pay put a drain on their coffers.

The situation with the Arabs had become far more stable by the beginning of the Macedonian Dynasty with an uneasy status quo setting in, which was not dissimilar to that which they had experienced with the Sassanid Persians in earlier centuries. Unlike the situation with Sassanids, the Byzantines were not crushed underfoot by the conquering Muslims under the initial assaults, but they were weakened greatly. As both sides settled into a pattern of launching raids against the other and then retaliating in kind, the Byzantines managed not to lose further significant territory to them until after this dynasty was finished.

A significant development came in the form of the newly emerged state of Kievan Rus in the ninth century. While it was initially yet another rival with which to war against, Kievan Rus, following its Christianization traditionally said to have occurred in 987 CE, became an ally of sorts and trading partner to the Byzantines. Though they fought repeatedly, often over the desire in Kiev to establish more favorable trade agreements, the Byzantines ended up holding a great deal of influence over the comparatively fledgling state. Their architectural style came to dominate in Kiev, their style of writing greatly influenced that of the Kievan elite, and their trade ties significantly helped to build up the eastern European polity.

One thing which greatly influenced their success in the next century was the shift in policy on the issue of Iconoclasm. While it had been woefully unpopular with Rome, that hadn't been the worst aspect of following the policy that they did for much of the eighth and ninth centuries. The cultural cost of Iconoclasm was immense as the policy called not just to ban people from worshiping with icons but for the icons themselves to be destroyed. Numerous works of Byzantine art were destroyed over the course of the period, with the policy remaining in place first from 730-783 CE and again from 814-842 CE. Curiously, in both instances, it was a Queen Regent ruling on behalf of a king still in his minority that ended it. The second time, under the regency of Queen Theodora, mother of Michael III, it was ended for good. During the reigns of both Michael III and Basil I, the people were free to create religious artwork again, contributing to the renaissance which had fed the period's revival.

The true height of the Macedonian period came under the reign of Basil II. Ruling from 976-1025 CE, Basil proved himself to be both a capable administrator and a ruthless general. As his father Romanos II died in 963 CE when Basil was only five years old, he was left unable to rule. Under the regencies of the general Nikephoros II and his nephew John I Tzimiskes, the pair became successive co-Emperors to the child. It was not until 976 CE that Basil came to rule alone, and by that point, the incompetence and administrative neglect of his co-Emperors had left the empire in a state of severe civil unrest. The wealthy Anatolian generals Bardas Skleros and Bardas Phokas both took up arms against the new Emperor, seeking to reduce him back to the powerless figurehead he had been under the reigns of Nikephoros II and John I.

Phokas was at first loyal to the new Emperor and served to help him put down Skleros' rebellion in 979 CE. When he, in turn, chose to rebel in 989 CE, however, his old enemy became his ally against Basil. In need of more allies, Basil entered negotiations with Vladimir I of Kievan Rus, who agreed to supply troops and supplies to the embattled Emperor and even convert both himself and his nation to Christianity in exchange for Basil's sister Anna's hand in marriage. This was an unprecedented move as the Byzantines, in true Roman fashion, had continued to see the various peoples of Europe outside their own domain as "barbarians." As his situation required sacrifice, however, Basil agreed, and after Phokas and Skleros had been dealt with in 989 CE, the promised pair were wed.

Beginning his reign under such unfavorable conditions had a profound impact on the still-young ruler, and advice apparently given by his old enemy seemed to have just as important an influence on Basil. According to the historian Psellus, after he was defeated, Bardas Skleros is said to have imparted on the young Basil the following:

> *"Cut down the governors who become over-proud. Let no generals on campaign have too many resources. Exhaust them with unjust exactions, to keep them busied with their own affairs. Admit no woman to the imperial councils. Be accessible to no one. Share with few your most intimate plans."*

Once the civil wars were finished, Basil II found himself needing to address a matter which had been impossible to see to since they began: the empire's external enemies. The

Fatamid Dynasty had taken full advantage of its enemy's internal strife and had seized back lands in Anatolia which Nikephoros II and John I had managed to reclaim. Over the next decade, Basil was forced to take to the field personally on numerous occasions against the Fatimids, initially in defense against the Emirate of Aleppo. Though neither side proved capable of achieving a decisive blow against the other, Basil held his own against the Muslim forces well enough that he managed to attain a lasting peace with them in 1000 CE. This secured his eastern front for the rest of his reign and allowed him time to focus on an issue which mattered far more to him: the Bulgarians.

Throughout Basil's reign, though he enjoyed great victories against the Georgians and the Khazars, no one was as devastated by the warrior Emperor than the Bulgarians. Earning himself the nickname "the Bulgar Slayer," Basil II managed to undertake an utterly crushing campaign against the Bulgarian Empire. While Basil was occupied with his civil wars and his wars in the east, Tsar Samuel of Bulgaria took advantage of the opportunity and conducted raids throughout Byzantine lands. Basil, having no desire to leave such a capable enemy so close to his European holdings, set out in 1000 CE with a force fit to raid and capture Bulgarian-held towns and fortresses. For the next eighteen years, he continued this pattern annually, slowly chipping away at the Bulgarian lands until they were ultimately all in his possession.

One particularly violent scenario from the war paints a picture of just how brutal Basil had become by the end of his reign. In 1014 CE, Basil and his general Nikephoros Xiphias routed and surrounded a Bulgarian army, capturing fifteen thousand men. The chronicles say that in his cruelty, he had ninety-nine out of every hundred men blinded, and left the final one with only one eye to lead the others home. The story went on that when Tsar Samuel saw the sight of his utterly destroyed army, it resulted in a stroke which killed him. Now, regardless of whether or not this is exaggerated, what is known for certain is that by the end of the Conquest of Bulgaria, Basil was so widely feared that Bulgaria's ally Croatia decided to accept his supremacy in the area for fear of facing his wrath if they did not.

Whether one sees him as a brutal butcher, a brilliant tactician, or both, what is certain is that by the end of Basil's reign in 1025 CE, the Byzantine Empire was at its absolute zenith in terms of power. Unlike the state, it was in at the end of the reign of Justinian I, its forces and resources were not overextended, and it had the power to hold onto what he had gained. He even left the treasury full of gold, a rarity for any wartime leader, let alone one who campaigned as frequently and enthusiastically as did Basil II. His reign was a good one, and he might well have been the most capable leader that the Empire ever had. But while the state of affairs in the Byzantine Empire was good when he died, that did not last long.

Chapter 5:
The Crusades and Their Impact

There is no shortage out there of books on the Crusades, as the subject has fascinated people throughout the west for centuries. Most of these, however, tend to focus on the crusades from the perspective of the Western Frankish forces who responded to the Papal call to arms. What is given somewhat less emphasis is the role played by the Byzantines both during the calls for help in the first place and during the conflicts themselves. To understand how the Byzantine Empire went from a position of strength in 1025 CE to needing to call for help in 1095 CE would require some explanation.

Basil II left the Byzantine Empire in the best shape it had ever been in after the fall of Rome. His brother Constantine VIII, who had technically been co-Emperor with him since they were so-named in 962 CE, had remained in the shadows, far away from governance due to a personal lack of interest in the concept. This lack of interest did not change after his brother's death, and since Basil died childless, his brother assumed the throne for the last three years of his own life. Constantine VIII was by all accounts a negligent and sadistic ruler whose brief reign is generally understood to have been a catastrophe. On his deathbed, with no son to pass the throne to, he attempted to give it to Constantine Dalessenus, a powerful aristocrat, by marrying the man to his daughter Zoe. He was then persuaded by court officials, who preferred a more easily controlled Emperor, to marry her instead to Romanos Argyros—it was he who succeeded Constantine VIII as Romanos III.

Romanos III reigned for six years, which ended when he died in what is generally assumed to have been an act of murder. He was then replaced by Michael IV, Empress Zoe's lover, who was in turn succeeded by his nephew Michael V whom Zoe adopted. She remained in power from 1028 CE until 1042 CE when Michael V tried to exile her. It resulted to a popular uprising took which removed him from power in Zoe's favor. She remained in power until her death in 1050 CE. Having married again, she was succeeded by her final husband, Constantine IX.

In all this time, none of the Empire's rulers came close to possessing her uncle's skill at administration or military matters, and through the decades of instability and intrigue, the running of the state ended in large part in the hands of civil servants who understood little of the task given them. The single biggest victim of this period was the Byzantine army, which had been exceptionally strong under Basil II, a man who was himself far too feared by the end of his reign to have any reason to fear his army. But the weak rulers of this period did fear the potential in the army for insurrection; thus, they decided to retire their remaining native troops and began to rely entirely on mercenaries.

In this time, they faced renewed troubles from Bulgarian rebels, the new incursions of the Normans who were beginning to strike against both Byzantine territory in Southern Italy and the Emirate of Sicily, and the Seljuk Turks in the east. Though they held off these threats for a time, by the 1090s, the Turks and Normans, in particular, were enjoying success against the weary and weakened Byzantines.

Worsening their position was the fact that by the mid-11th century, the schism between the churches in the west and the churches in the east was complete. What was truly a slow-building dispute between the two sides came to a head in 1054 CE. There were numerous doctrinal disputes at the heart of the schism, most notably a dispute over the wording of the Nicene Creed, an important statement of belief used in both eastern and western liturgy. At the heart of the schism, however, was an increasing and mutual resentment on both sides for the other's claim to authority. This divide had been building since the end of the Byzantine Papacy in 752 CE and became more formal following the mutual excommunications of Pope Leo IX and Patriarch Michael I Cerularius. Even in the face of the Norman invasion of southern Italy which threatened Constantinople and Rome, the two sides could not come together to find a solution.

The 1071 CE Battle of Manzikert was a crushing defeat for the Byzantines and marked the first time in their history that a Byzantine Emperor, Romanos IV, was captured by a Muslim commander. It lost them significant control and power over Anatolia and pushed them back further than they had been in decades. Twenty years later, under Emperor Alexios I, the Byzantines won a brutal victory at the Battle of Levounion but were left in a vexing position. With the death of Robert Guiscard of the Normans in 1085 CE and the death of the Turkish Sultan the next year, that victory should have put Alexios I in a position to retake significant lost land. Unfortunately, he lacked the troops to accomplish that task. Seventy years of bureaucratic incompetence had left the Byzantine Empire's defenses in tatters. Though Alexios did work to rebuild the Byzantine army, it did not progress quickly enough to match his desires.

In a position to strike against his enemy but needing allies desperately, Alexios turned to Rome. Alexios knew how formidable the soldiers in the west could be from the Byzantine's encounters with the Normans in Italy. Hoping to capitalize on that, he sent ambassadors to request aid from the western kingdoms. At the Council Piacenza in 1095 CE, his ambassadors managed to make their appeal, and it ended up being more successful than he ever dreamed or wanted. The council had been called at the end of a tour through Italy and France conducted by Pope Urban II to reassert his authority after a drawn-out conflict with the Holy Roman Emperor Henry IV over which of the two had the right to appoint local church officials.

Due to the importance of the council, it was quite well-attended, needing to be held outside the city of Piacenza because two hundred bishops, four thousand church officials, and thirty thousand laymen were in attendance. When Alexios' ambassadors made their plea to help, emphasizing the suffering of Eastern Christians at the hands of the Turks, it moved their listeners, none more so than the Pope himself. Urban II urged all who were present to aid the Byzantines however way they could.

That same year, Urban II called the Council of Clermont in France and begged all who attended to do their part in striking against the infidels in the formerly Christian lands. The response was immense and well beyond the scope of anything that Alexios had likely had in mind when he first called for aid. Rather than a small disciplined mercenary army, he gained the help of thousands of undisciplined zealots, each seeking more to strike against the enemy than to follow the direction of Constantinople. That the first of these armies, a ragtag group led by the priest Peter the Hermit in 1096 CE, had been led to their slaughter in Nicaea was a perfect example of this.

When the armies led by experienced commanders arrived, they were more useful than Peter's force but no more willing to work for the Byzantine Emperor. Led by Godfrey of Boullion, the crusaders were sent by Alexios into Asia, along with a promise of provisions in exchange for oaths of loyalty. Though he did reclaim numerous cities along the Mediterranean coast through their efforts, the Crusaders came to see their oaths as having been made invalid by the fact that Alexios did not fight alongside them, particularly in their siege of Antioch.

Though the Byzantine Empire did regain most of western Anatolia, the Crusader's conquests in the Levant were taken by the princes and turned into the Levantine Crusader States. These were private kingdoms carved out of the Christian Holy Land which were to be administrated as Latin Rite states, opposing both the eastern Christians and the Muslims in the region. That most of the crusaders returned home after the crusade was finished in 1099 CE meant that these states were left vulnerable and arguably doomed to fail.

For his part, Alexios was left regretful for having called in the western soldiers in the first place. The First Crusade was an overwhelming success for much the same reason that the initial Muslim Conquests had been: the Muslim forces in the area, due in this case to division and infighting, were exhausted and ill-prepared for a well-executed military campaign when they first arrived. Over just three years, the Crusaders managed to take back more land than Christendom as a whole had held in the area in centuries. What this meant was that, though the Crusaders had accomplished all that they did and left, the fighting was certain to become significantly less one-sided once the Muslims in the area, particularly the Turks, managed to reorganize themselves. This is what happened leading up to the Second Crusade, as the reorganized Turks launched their counter-attack.

Though the First Crusade's ending was not ideal for the Byzantines, it still gave the weary empire room to breathe and recover. One could argue that internal incompetence had done more damage to the Byzantine Empire in the 11th century than had the Turks, and it was fortunate for them that they managed to avoid such problems for decades after the First Crusade. Alexios I was succeeded in 1118 CE by his son John II. John was a leader so bizarrely pious and good-tempered by Byzantine standards that he came to be known as John the Good. It was recorded that never once during his reign did he have anyone executed or blinded, and it was not for a lack of opportunity what with him having reigned for twenty-five years. He has been referred to as the Byzantine Marcus Aurelius, and not without reason. His reign was characterized by social revival and military accomplishment, with territories lost due to the Battle of Manzikert being reclaimed and garrisoned. He left the empire in 1143 CE with a full treasury and the prospect of a bright future. As was often the case with the Byzantine Empire, however, this was not to last.

Manuel, I reigned from 1143-1180 CE in what was arguably the final good period of the Byzantine Empire. His accomplishments were few and, as with many Byzantine Emperors, his ambition far exceeded his ability. He was unsuccessful in reclaiming southern Italy or the Anatolian interior, as he attempted. What he did succeed in doing, however, was weathering the Second Crusade. The Turks struck back against the Christian states in 1144 CE, decades after their defeat in the First Crusade, and captured the county of Edessa in eastern Anatolia. In response, the Crusaders launched the Second Crusade in 1147 CE. Unlike the first Crusade, they were not facing disorganized and war-weary armies, and the difference in the results was noteworthy.

The Second Crusade was a decisive victory for the Muslims who held onto Edessa and managed to get a peace treaty with the Byzantines, securing the territorial change. It set up the Fall of Jerusalem in 1187 CE, which would result in the Third Crusade that would end in much the same way. The Third Crusade would occur from 1189-1192 CE. It would see the Crusaders retake much of the Levantine coast as well as capture the island of Cyprus but fall short of their ultimate goal of reclaiming Jerusalem. In both cases, the two Christian groups came to feel as though the other had failed them, worsening relations. In truth, both defeats were the result of the growing divide caused by the East-West Schism and the continuing political tensions between the rival powers in the region. The worsening of relations between the Byzantines and the Latin states would result in easily the most cataclysmic event in the empire's history.

Chapter 6:
The Fourth Crusade

In history, you can find examples of unforced errors, unfortunate miscalculations, and unmitigated catastrophes which continue to perplex and mystify people to the present times. The Fourth Crusade, one of the last ones, was without a doubt the most unfortunate moment for the Byzantine Empire in its history, save for its final collapse. Though it was ultimately the Latin Crusaders who dealt the grievous blow to the Byzantine Empire, the empire itself was far from blameless for the position that they found themselves in.

When Manuel I died in 1180 CE, his eleven-year-old son Alexios II was left in power under the regency of his mother Maria of Antioch. Maria was of Frankish background and was unpopular as a consequence given the general sentiments toward the Latin west in Constantinople in the late 12th century. Alexios himself was but a boy and incapable of ruling on his own. Thus, his uncle Andronikos, in 1182 CE, led a popular uprising against Maria and installed himself as co-Emperor. During this uprising, he also led the Massacre of the Latins, wherein the city's thousands of Latin inhabitants were slaughtered almost to a man. The westerners in the city had grown wealthy, and jealousy was quite likely a factor in the brutal act. The strain this placed on relations with the west was both considerable and unsurprising.

Andronikos then went farther in 1183 CE by having the child Emperor strangled and marrying his twelve-year-old betrothed Agnes of France. The nobility in the Byzantine Empire had grown more powerful under the rule of Manuel I and, fearing their strength, Andronikos sought to suppress their power. His measures were characteristically brutal as he sought to wipe out anyone who might be powerful enough to try to take the throne from him. In 1185 CE, he ordered that all prisoners and their families be executed for the crime of colluding with foreign invaders, leading to a number of riots.

Amidst all of this, William II of Sicily decided to take advantage of the chaos and invade the Byzantine territory, capturing and pillaging the city of Thessalonica. When Andronikos sailed out to prevent the Normans from making further gains in his territory, Issac Angelos, the son of a military leader in Anatolia, killed Andronikos' lieutenant Stephen Hagiochristophorites and pleaded with the people of Constantinople to help him end the madness. Andronikos returned to the city to find that Issac II had been proclaimed Emperor, and though he did try to flee, he was captured and given to an angry mob who, according to accounts from the time, tore him apart.

Issac II reigned for ten years, at the end of which he was deposed and blinded by his older brother Alexios III. It was a Byzantine Empire in this state of disunion and chaos which the Crusaders found when the Fourth Crusade began.

The Third Crusade was more successful for the Crusaders than the Second Crusade had been, but as with the Second Crusade, it failed to achieve its primary goal. In the case of the Third Crusade, that goal had been the reclamation of Jerusalem which had fallen to the forces of Saladin in 1187 CE. That desire to recapture the heart of the Holy Land was still strong in 1198 CE, just six years after the end of the Third Crusade when Pope Innocent III first called for a new Crusade. Innocent III had ascended to the Papacy earlier that same year and was eager to renew the fight for Christendom.

There were a few key differences right from the start between this Crusade and those which had preceded it. For one thing, it had been less than a decade since the forces of Europe had gone to war with the Muslims, and fatigue was still quite prevalent across the continent. It was largely due to this that when Innocent III issued his Papal Bull *Post miserabile* in 1198 CE, it went almost entirely ignored. Another possible factor for this was the changing attitudes in the west toward the Greek Christians. The Crusades had brought the two sides closer together than they had been for centuries, and there was precious little that was lost in cultural translation. The Byzantines, having been forced to deal directly with the Muslim powers on their virtual doorstep, had been forced to negotiate with them from time to time. The Latin Christians, who had enjoyed the luxury of distance and did not understand this, saw the willingness to treat with their religious enemy as a betrayal of the faith. The Massacre of the Latins just a few years prior had also done little to improve the image of the Byzantines in their eyes.

Fulk of Neuilly, a popular French preacher, managed through his sermons in 1099 CE to convince Count Thibaut of Champagne to organize a tournament meant to shore up support for Innocent's crusade. He did so, and with enough support gathered for the venture, it was decided that they would avoid having to cross all the way through the Byzantine Empire and Anatolia by sailing instead to Egypt. A strike against Jerusalem from the south, they figured, would give them a strategic advantage. To that end, it was decided to approach the Venetians for the commissioning of a fleet, and Thibault was elected leader of the Crusade. When he died two years later, the leadership role was taken over by Boniface of Montferrat.

The Venetians were reluctant to get involved, but by 1201 CE, they had been persuaded to create a fleet capable of transporting thirty-three thousand, five hundred troops to Egypt for a cost of eighty-five thousand silver marks. When the crusaders arrived a year later with only twelve thousand troops and only thirty-five thousand silver marks, the Venetians threatened to keep the fleet, but they could ill-afford to do so given the vast cost of creating it. When the Doge of Venice, Enrico Dandolo, suggested that the Crusaders pay off their debt by besieging the city of Zara, some refused to do so and left, but the bulk of the army agreed to the terms.

Zara was a Catholic city which had been under the dominion of Venice for many years but had, in 1181 CE, rebelled and joined King Emeric of Hungary and Croatia in an alliance. Hungary too was a Catholic kingdom, and so, the Fourth Crusade began not by attacking a Muslim port or even a Byzantine port but one belonging to a fellow Latin Christian state. The siege did not last long with the Crusaders arriving by the 11th of November 1202 CE and entering the city by the 24th. The pillaging which followed horrified Innocent III who sent a letter threatening to excommunicate the entire army if they did not make their way to Jerusalem immediately. The leaders of the Crusade, however, not wanting to negatively impact morale, neglected to share that information.

While the Crusaders were in Zara, Boniface of Montferrat, having managed to slip away before the fleet left Venice, decided to visit his cousin, Philip of Swabia. Philip happened to be hosting Alexios Angelos, the son of the recently deposed Issac II of the Byzantine Empire. While there, Alexios promised to cover the debt owed to the Venetians, give an additional two hundred thousand silver marks to the crusaders, send ten thousand Byzantine professional troops to assist with the Crusade, and place the Eastern Church under Papal authority if they would help overthrow Alexios III and restore his father to the throne. Boniface was more than happy to relay this information to his fellow Crusaders who, in turn, found it an impossibly tempting offer. Though already having angered the Pope by attacking a Christian city, Alexios' offer turned out to be too good to turn down even with the possibility of Innocent's wrath.

The siege began on July 11th of 1203 CE, with the Venetian fleet having managed to cross the Bosporus Strait with relative ease. As the Venetian army retreated behind their walls, the Venetian siege weapons managed to start a fire which spread through one hundred and twenty acres of the city. As Alexios III rushed out to meet them, his army outnumbered them by more than two to one. The surprise attack and raging fire stole his nerve, however, and the entire army retreated back behind the walls. Disgraced and seeking a way out, Alexios had his loyalists seize as much gold as they could and fled the city. As the city officials realized what had happened, they moved quickly to depose Alexios formally and restored Issac II to the throne. The Crusaders were left in a quandary in that they had achieved their goals but realized that the man who had made them such tempting promises was not sitting on the throne. They refused to accept Issac's rule unless his son was named co-Emperor as Alexios IV and the officials, wanting the siege to end, agreed.

Upon taking power, Alexios quickly realized that there was little to no way for him to keep his promises. For one thing, Alexios III had taken around one thousand pounds of gold and jewels with him when he fled the city, and even if he had not, he had still spent the last eight years spending the empire into the ground. As he turned to destroying icons to salvage the gold in the hopes of paying the Latin army off with them, the people quickly turned on him. Within the year, he was killed and replaced by a courier named Alexios Doukas—who took the reign name Alexios V—and was quickly followed by his father who died of natural causes. The Crusaders were incensed at the death of their would-be patron and quickly moved to take what they felt they were owed by force.

The Sack of Constantinople in 1204 CE occurred on April 13th of that year and lasted for three days. The pillaging is said to have gained for the Crusaders over nine hundred thousand silver marks' worth of treasure, and they burned and looted with reckless abandon. It is said that they even seated a prostitute on the throne of the Orthodox Patriarch as a particular attack on the Greek Orthodox Church. When Innocent III heard of it, he was horrified and rebuked them in no uncertain terms, but there was little that he could do. The Byzantine Empire had fallen, and in its place, the Crusaders raised the Latin Empire.

The Latin Empire was an attempt to supplant the Byzantine Empire as the Roman Empire in the east, with the hope being that under the rule of Roman Catholics, it would in time become a Catholic state. It was ill-conceived from the start and, in the end, only lasted until 1261 CE. In a way, the eventually successful Byzantines had their old enemy the Bulgarians to thank for the ability to take the empire back from the Latins, as they warred with the Latin Empire constantly in the hopes of securing their own gains. In addition, the Empire of Nicaea formed by Byzantine nobles following the capture of Constantinople from their old territory in western Anatolia continued to raid the rump state throughout the decades following its creation. By 1250 CE, the Niceans had taken almost all of the territory surrounding the city back, and over the next eleven years and after numerous attempts, they managed to break down the resolve of the defenders. In 1261 CE, the city fell again to the people who had ruled it for nearly a thousand years. But though they had managed to take back their city, there was little that could be done to truly restore their old empire.

Chapter 7:
The Decline of the Empire and the Fall of Constantinople

The devastation caused in 1204 CE had a long-term and ultimately fatal impact on the Byzantine Empire. Even after retaking the city in 1261 CE, the Byzantines found themselves in a permanent state of decline which was only worsened by the infighting which came to define the 14th century. Worse than this was the fact that by the end of the 13th century, the Byzantine Empire found itself not only reduced to the smallest state it had ever been in but also surrounded by increasingly powerful enemies.

In the absence of a strong power based in Constantinople, the Serbians began to assert themselves in the Balkan region. The Kingdom of Serbia first emerged in 1217 CE, more than a decade after Constantinople fell. At its peak, during the Serbian imperial period under Stefan IV Dusan, it spanned much of modern-day Serbia, Montenegro, Greece, and Albania, having taken much of what was known to the Byzantines as the region of Epirus from the empire while it was under Latin occupation. By the end of Stefan's reign in 1355 CE, they also held much of formerly Byzantine Macedonia, depriving the once-powerful empire of land which held major cultural and economic significance to them.

The Bulgarians also reasserted themselves in this era, managing to reclaim much of the territory they had once held before their conquest at the hands of Basil II. The Second Bulgarian Empire came to be in 1185 CE, during the disastrous reign of Andronikos I and before the Fourth Crusade. Despite this, it was not until after their victory in the 1205 CE Battle of

Adrianople over the Latin Empire that they began to reclaim their status as a regional power. At their peak, during the reign of Ivan Asen II in the early to mid-13th century, their territory spanned from the Black Sea coast of modern Bulgaria and Romania through to Macedonia. Conflicts with their neighboring states and internal strife would halt their advance, but in the end, as was the case with Serbia and eventually the Byzantine Empire as well, what truly caused the decline of Bulgaria was the rise of the most consequential regional power of the day, the Ottoman Turks.

The Seljuk Turks, united under the Sultanate of Rum, had been the primary Turkish power in Anatolia for over two centuries when the Ottomans first rose to prominence in 1299 CE. They were the primary power in the region that the Crusaders had fought against and with whom the Byzantines had signed a treaty with at the end of the Second Crusade. By the end of the 13th century, however, they were undeniably in decline. The fact that they failed to take full advantage of the chaos caused by the brief Latin Empire was proof enough of that. The Ottomans, however, starting under their first leader Osman I, grew rapidly from a small and insignificant Emirate to the most powerful Muslim state in the world. Little is known of Osman himself as Ottoman records at the time were not extensive. His son Orhan, however, was the Sultan who captured the city of Bursa in Modern Turkey, the emirate's first major capital.

Over the course of the 14th century, the Ottomans managed to capture much of Anatolia and the Balkans, so much so that by the turn of the 15th century, the Byzantine empire was surrounded on all sides. Their advance into Europe was made possible by their capture of Gallipoli in 1354 CE. This victory was made easy for them by an earthquake which struck that year, devastating the local fort in the region. With the Byzantines tied up in their own internal struggles at the time, they were unable to refortify in time to prevent the Ottomans from gaining their bridge into Europe. The 1389 CE Battle of Kosovo ended the Serbian Empire and gave the Ottomans control over most of the land surrounding Constantinople. By 1402 CE, their conquests in the area were nearly complete, and the situation for the city of Constantinople looked bleak. Their situation was not entirely the result of poor luck and circumstance, however. Rather, they did much to ensure that they had little if any chance of stopping the advancing threat of the Ottomans.

There were two major civil wars fought in the Byzantine Empire during the 14th century. The first, lasting from 1321-1328 CE, was fought between Emperor Andronikos II and his grandson who desired the throne for himself. It was drawn out and not entirely conclusive, with his grandson ending up named co-Emperor as Andronikos III, but it was important for what it meant for the world surrounding the empire. It was during this time, in 1326 CE, that Orhan managed to capture Bursa, a city in Anatolia less than one hundred kilometers away from Constantinople itself, and made it his capital. Vast swaths of Anatolian territory was lost in this time due to the Byzantine Empire's distraction. When Andronikos III died in 1341 CE, it sparked another civil war which lasted until 1347 CE. This civil war permitted the Serbian Empire to seize significant territory in Macedonia and Epirus, again barely facing any challenge.

Both of these civil wars were, at their hearts, conflict between the increasingly powerful aristocrats and either the central government or the people at large. They both speak of an empire which was openly in decline and whose people had come to focus inward due to there being little point in looking outward. It is impossible to say for certain that the empire would have had any chance of halting the advance of their enemies, especially the Ottomans if they had not been so caught up in their own distraction. It is entirely possible that they were simply left too weak following the rise and fall of the Latin Empire to make a difference. What is certain, however, is that the Ottomans were greatly assisted by the disorganization and chaos found in their enemies when they began taking the Balkans by force.

In 1402 CE, with the Byzantine Empire left a mere shell of its former self, it was holding as its territory just the city of Constantinople itself and a small stretch of land to the west. Despite this, the Ottomans still struggled to take the city due to its continuing strategic advantage. The Bosporus Strait and the famous walls of the city were still formidable defenses, even if the city they sheltered was increasingly a dilapidated husk. The Byzantines were given unwitting aid in 1302 CE, however, when the Turko-Mongol leader Timur invaded Anatolia from the east. Timur was the founder of the Timurid Dynasty and desired more than anything to restore the old empire of Genghis Khan. A devout Muslim, Timur justified his invasions of powers such as the Ottomans as a necessary work to remove usurpers and restore proper Mongol rule. The Battle of Ankara in 1402 CE resulted in a crushing defeat for the Ottomans, and the capture of Sultan Bayezid I. What resulted from that was a civil war over which of the Sultan's sons would take power, and it raged until 1413 CE when Mehmed I took the throne.

The Ottoman civil war did result in the temporary loss of some territories such as Kosovo and Thessaloníki, but these losses did not last long. For Constantinople, their primary problem in the 14th century was a lack of manpower. Their city, which had at one point been the largest in Europe, had declined greatly under the weight of frequent attacks. Since 1261 CE, it had withstood assaults from the Latins, the Bulgarians, the Serbians, and the Turks, but with so little land to help sustain it, its population had suffered. In 1453 CE, when the final conquest occurred, the city managed to gather together a defensive force of seven thousand men, two thousand of which were from the west. Not helping this was the Black Plague, which had affected the city a century earlier, from 1343-1346 CE.

Efforts were made on the Byzantines' part to seek help from the west, but the Latin powers were reluctant to give it unless the people converted to the Latin Rite which they simply were not willing to do, even in the face of almost-certain defeat. That is not to say that no one in the west desired to help defend the city—thousands did volunteer—but the numbers paled in comparison to what was needed. When the siege began, the total population of the city stood at around fifty thousand people, with the invading Ottoman Army exceeding even that number. Though their situation was dire and aid seemed unlikely at best, it did not stop the final Byzantine Emperor, Constantine XI, from doing all that he could to shore up the defenses.

Constantine knew that the invasion was coming and did all that was possible to prevent the fall of the city. First, he had the walls first constructed on the order of Theodosius II repaired and reinforced; then he gathered all of the supplies and troops that he could for the defense. With so little land, money, and time, however, his best efforts ended up being paltry. In the end, he led a force of seven thousand troops against an army ten times its size. There was in all likelihood no amount of preparations capable of turning the tide on that battle.

The Ottoman forces were led by the ambitious young Sultan Mehmed II, who would thereafter be known as Mehmed the Conqueror. He began his siege on April 6th of 1453 CE, and by May 29th the same year, it was finished, with Mehmed having accomplished what countless other would-be conquerors before him had failed to do: taking one of the most prized cities in the world. The first several assaults on the walls themselves ended as most others had before. Mehmed's losses were significant, and his advisors more than once became split on the subject of whether or not to continue the siege. On May 21st, he sent an envoy to Constantine XI, offering him and anyone else willing to do so the opportunity to flee with their goods and their lives intact. Constantine rebuked the offer, however, indicating that he intended to die in the defense of the city if that was what it came down to. On the 29th, after remobilizing his forces, Mehmed ordered the final assault. Throwing the bulk of his forces against the walls in waves, the onslaught turned out to be too much for the weary and depleted defenders to deal with.

Accounts differ on whether Constantine hanged himself during the final battle or removed his imperial regalia and charged with his men in one last futile stand, but regardless of which is true, by the end of the day, the final Byzantine Emperor was dead, and the city Constantine the Great had rededicated in 330 CE had fallen. It would thereafter become the capital of the rapidly expanding Ottoman Empire, remaining as such until its own fall in 1922 CE.

With that fall, there remained little left of the old Byzantine Empire. The independent states of Trebizond and Epirus, which came into being after the creation of the Latin Empire in 1204, continued on for a time, but by the end of the 15th century, they had also been conquered by the Ottomans. If one considers the Byzantine Empire to have been the continuation of the Roman Empire all the way to the end, as many do, then the death of Constantine XI and the fall of Constantinople represented the final fall of Rome itself. An empire started in 27 BCE by Emperor Augustus lived on in one form or another until that day, and so it was that a nearly fifteen-thousand-year chapter of history came to a close.

Conclusion

Thank you for making it through to the end of *The Byzantine Empire: A Thousand Year History from Start to Finish*. Let's hope it was informative and helped you understand more about the history of one of the most fascinating empires in human history. The highs and lows of the incredibly inconsistent empire have intrigued people to this day. Just because you've finished the book, however, does not mean your move to learn more about the Byzantine Empire has to stop here.

If you want to learn more about the empire, its culture, its history, or anything else about it, there are plenty of further resources out there to help you. From documentary series to college lectures to other books, there are innumerable ways to seek out more and more information. It's difficult to fit a full millennium of history into any one book, and there are still plenty of materials out there to be learned. University professors who specialize in the subject have spent their whole lifetimes researching the empire and still keep finding new things about it.

Whether one wants to dedicate their lives to the study of this interesting period of history or just learn more for their own enjoyment and entertainment, the history of the Byzantine Empire contains no shortage of stories both epic and occasionally bizarre to amuse and inform people to this day.

Finally, if you found this book useful in any way, a review is always appreciated!

www.ingramcontent.com/pod-product-compliance
Lightning Source LLC
Chambersburg PA
CBHW052209110526
44591CB00012B/2141